BEC
SOUND OF BEES

BY
MARC VINCENZ

AMPERSAND BOOKS

AMPERSAND BOOKS
www.ampersand-books.com

ISBN: 978-0-9861370-0-6

Cover design by Matthew Revert
Cover art: Henryk Fantazos © 2014, "Beekeepers' Dance"
Interior design by Kelvin Carlos

OTHER BOOKS BY MARC VINCENZ

Poetry:

The Propaganda Factory, or Speaking of Trees

Gods of a Ransacked Century

Mao's Mole

Behind the Wall at the Sugar Works (a verse novel)

Additional Breathing Exercises
(bilingual German-English selected poems)

Beautiful Rush

This Wasted Land and Its Chymical Illuminations
(with Tom Bradley)

Translations:

Kissing Nests (translations of Werner Lutz)

Nightshift / An Area of Shadows
(translations of Erika Burkart and Ernst Halter)

Grass Grows Inward (translations of Andreas Neeser)

Out of the Dust (translations of Klaus Merz)

A Late Recognition of the Signs (translations of Erika Burkart)

PRAISE FOR
BECOMING THE SOUND OF BEES

& the sky was birdless//we listened//for the sound of bees

In the search for illumination, navigational lines transmute to brinks, horizons, loss; leaving the visionary to his intentional muse, a specific, dream-keen concise dead-reckoning splitting some supreme immortal blur. Here, Vincenz graces poetic bounty with waving rhythm, stirs a ruffling of ocean into sheets spread between man and more, giving us our own mortal reflection and calling us to sail. *Becoming the Sound of Bees* masterfully portrays the quest for truth in a journey ripe with the child-scrawl of angels, winged-spiders, honeyguides and honeybirds traversing the globe to locate home, and in this voyage brings a hero's heart. Exemplary—

—Allison Adelle Hedge Coke, author of *Streaming*
and winner of the American Book Award

What a startlingly powerful collection this is. Vincenz's *Becoming the Sound of Bees*, takes the reader to that vibratory level where narrative and the resonant energy of language are in continuous transformation. We are moved through veil after veil of the mundane then in and out of the tarnished glimmer of what might be otherworldly. The feminine figurations of oceans, daughters, wives are raved at by the iconic masculine prototype Ivan who dares "to scream Blue at the sea." Frail universes build, crest, and capsize. Yet we are given exacting details from myth, history, science, and anthropology that fly by us humming, only to sink and collide seemingly in the same breath. The musical quality of Vincenz's gorgeous language is remarkable; the narrative of a ruined earth is urgent. Yet always there appears a lucid gem of what might be (or once was), and it is in this "becoming" we discover a redeeming focus on singularity. The poem "The Sign, The Symbol, The Bird" offers such visual vigor in the flight of a simple thrush: "that flash of speckled feather resting at intervals on threadbare scrub," only to "whistle back into her own marvelous concoction." This collection is captivating both for its unique use of language and for the breadth, depth, and clarity of the narrative.

—Katherine Soniat, author of *The Swing Girl*

Becoming the Sound of Bees is the music, the mind and muscle of a poet intimately engaged with the world becoming, with Being taking shape and presence. It is a fractured cinematic narrative where scenes saturate one another and characters shift and exchange faces, some of which are our own—such is the strength of its hold on the imagination. It is history (personal and communal) through kaleidoscopic mind, keenly aware that any event might open an unexpected portal into any other. It is trans-figuration out of the body toward infinite forms more real than symbols, more tangible than myth, yet ripe with the plenitude of both those modes. It is a book of physical knowledge as reveled by a natural philosopher in the ancient sense and a magician in the modern sense. It may be read as a collection of poems, but beneath that appearance lies a continuum, a singer sounding the depths and making finely articulated open verse out of the torrent of experience.

—Jake Berry, author of *Brambu Drezi*

In *Becoming the Sound of Bees*, Marc Vincenz's "facts of mind made manifest / in a fiction of matter" capture the process of transformation as it occurs in daily life, personal reflection and philosophical ideation. His sharp eye and deft hand capture shifts of perception that apprehend experience through language or as a manifestation of language itself. Provocative, beautiful, unsettling and highly recommended.

—Vernon Frazer, author of *Unsettled Music*

Marc Vincenz's poetry is stellar. *Becoming the Sound of Bees* is a truly amazing collection—linguistically rich, complex, musical and critically precise in its engagement with the felt wor(l)d."

—David Wolf, author of *Sablier* and *Sablier II*

Persuasive, pensive and experimental, in the best sense of that overused term, the poems in *Becoming the Sound of Bees* engage with a world that only seems as if it is failing us. In the appropriately titled, "Continuum," Vincenz says "that a creator may/draw strings and each and every/last one may last/beyond the great oblivion/at the end of all things." Other poems are entitled, "Yet Another Reincarnation," "Godwilling," and "After the Greatest War." Through static, storms, panic and cacophony, Vincenz's poems emerge with a rhythmic, assonant, euphonious song that just might be a path toward salvation. This is a book of hope and vision that is uncommon because it is hard-won and true. Thanks are due Marc Vincenz for his clear-eyed farsightedness.

—Corey Mesler, author of *The Catastrophe of my Personality*

Marc Vincenz is a genuine poet, not something you can say of very many poets these days. He belongs to the generation that is in ascendancy, as the older generations are fading in interest and influence, and it would be foolish not to be aware of his work.

—Ben Mazer, *Battersea Review*

In *Becoming the Sound of Bees*, our greatest social and environmental fears are realized and Vincenz's narrators are timeless witnesses to a post-apocalyptic world, following "the fine threads that spin between illusion / and legend and history and the distance / that is only measured in trees and birds and ghosts " ("Instructions on Following a Calling"). But Marc Vincenz's poems are anything but wispy or ethereal. They are visually cinematic allegories that engage a reader in surprisingly forceful ways.

—James Cervantes, *The Salt River Review*

Marc Vincenz's *Becoming the Sound of Bees* is visionary, poised between nightmare and dream, and convincing. The poems give us a narrative that collapses narrative, characters that collapse character, a sense of past, present, and future that collapses time. But even within this sense of things falling apart, I read a sense of construction—is it the fact that, with all hope abandoned, the poems continue? That, in a mythological and ritualized landscape warp and woof, they demand reading? Is that the hope they offer? I don't know. I only know my certainty that *Becoming the Sound of Bees* is powerful and demanding, radiating like a dark star.

—Mark Statman, author of *A Map of the Winds*

Animated by thought, matter and antimatter, *Becoming the Sound of Bees* churns through rediscovered worlds. As you reach the end, you realize that this book is a collective metamorphosis, a "becoming." The result is a rude awakening. This is a book for the ages; should be highly lauded and strongly recommended.

—Ron Kolm, *Evergreen Review*

Within an expanding and contracting poetry—the mystical Ivan, scrapping fisherman or sea satyr, wonders amid the language of loss and despair and an ever-warring hope—"… behind the walls a million oracles waiting."—A mystical unraveling and unveiling—"… billowing into an oven of gold, or the unrelenting hands of anti-matter …"—Vincenz's poetry evokes worlds of detail anchored through figures of power and perpetual demise who are most humble and common, wise and dangerous—and capable of a Dostoevskyisan consciousness and suffering. Rather than a poetry of anger and retaliation, Vincenz's poetry trawls the realms of existential crises, hope and possible redemption—but only within a purview of this nature's passionately quotidian terms.

—George J. Farrah, author of *The Low Pouring Stars*

One might think that *Becoming the Sound of Bees* would entail mixing with the white noise of the natural world and miss the specific symmetries and orchestral richness of that world's hidden, vital communications. Since bees are the landscape architects of the American pastoral story, their purpose is intrinsic to our planet's survival. Vincenz slowly unravels all the grace notes of this necessary mission with his own unfailing music and pollinates the reader's imagination with a host of metaphorical associations. His narratives illustrate the impossible odds of true human interaction and shows us how poetry can provide the improbable solutions inside the human hive, where all bets are off. In the lava roll of his imagination, Vincenz's poems uncover the tender places where we might reconnect. In a variety of shapes and rhythms, he makes of this book a balm that heals the wounds we inflict upon one another, and the natural world, by virtue of all our appetites and reasons. This book is a powerful reminder of just why poetry is what the world really wants when its heart is broken.

—Keith Flynn, *Asheville Poetry Review*

Listen to this:

> Abut in a tailspin, mad
> spark of keratin scratching hard-
> wood
>
> —and that buck-
> toothed back
> -bite, double-
>
> chew driving through
> everything if-you
> -pleases:

And this:

> Now again,
>
> the seas begin to rise; each day the tide falls in closer
> reclaiming more of the land, I postulate that soon we
> shall have to live on stilts like the Bajau Laut tribes of Semporna
> who built their homes on coral reefs in the ocean ...

And tell me you would recognize immediately that these are passages by the same author, in the same book. I wouldn't have. But they are. Such is Marc Vincenz's range—from the light touch of Language poetry to the straightforward narrative (though not for long) of the second piece. And more styles in between and more perspectives and astonishments—all handled with the same mastery, if one can say that over-used word. He has read everything, and most of it makes an appearance (surprising but always necessary) somewhere in *Becoming the Sound of Bees*: from the Stasi to Wang's Golden Wok, the soul-umbrella to shin-yapping hounds to dust-dreaming-up fog, and the snowfall ... and these but almost-at-random of rust and paint and broken nails—And so much more.

Yes, a rare and rarified beauty here. Vincenz has ransacked the hives and offers us the honey, dripping from his fingers. Take it.

—Daniel Lawless, Editor, *Plume*

TABLE OF CONTENTS

THREE

FOUR

BECOMING THE
SOUND OF BEES

BY

MARC VINCENZ

life is the germ

—Louis Pasteur

TRANSMIGRATION

—for Yves Bonnefoy

Hunchbacked we knock
heads, trying not to feel

the other's fingers as the sea cuts
and tugs and urges, muffling

in its flabby, swollen girth.
The dampness seethes, squeezes

into that rough gravity
of curved planks. Salt encases

hair, a second skin
where indentations,

crevices or scars trace icons
of a recurring past, crystal heaped

in ions as fleas creep into our rags
and rats' eyes quiver like insect eggs.

Voices are rigging and sails
that creak and snap, and through

knots and cracks above, the light,
finding little access, ceaselessly bemoans.

And when we emerge, some of us less
than half the men we once knew,

in one blinding flash, as dog greets master,
that curious light comes running. And then,

hovering for a split second, panting
over a torn scrap of cloth,

a flapping shoe sole, continues,
right out the other side.

ONE

STATIC

In that year
that was not a year

when the days
were not like days

& the sky was bird-
less
        we listened

for the sound of bees
& hearing nothing

but the wind box the panes
we began to hum & buzz & drone

becoming the grey matter
before words

IMAGO

& within the head within the heart within the skin there are no wishes
                                                                all the flavor
has left his tongue & anything of worth has been burned
                                                        leaving
nothing but singed nerve-endings that hum when it rains or
                                                        when
a lightning storm approaches & in that moment he tosses in his bed
                                                        wraps
his damp sheets around like bandages presses his legs into his chest
                                                        until again
the moment passes the air becomes thin & he slips into his pupa
                                                        waiting to
awaken in his new hard shell praying the gods will grant him wings

IVAN SINKS INTO THE HONEYCOMB

After all his yowls and cajoles,
Ivan has lost his chords
and sinks into the shallows,
into the impressions

of mollusks and seasnails,
hangs his head in his hands
as if he wants to hold on to it.
He knows what I think of him,

the hoarder of things he once was,
the hoarder of memories he has become.
It's too heavy, he mutters
as if to the spinning minnows

and the jellied eggs of crustaceans
yet to become.
And what of Tatjana, he mumbles
scratching a face in the sand;

the shadow of the wall
now hovers over his skull like a hive
burning alive in honeybees—
as if I had answers

as if I might become
soothsayer, groundbreaker
(when all that's left is you,
you become everything or nothing).

If only we'd always lived cut-
off on an island, he spits,
sinking into the honeycomb,
drifting far away from me.

STORM CLOUD

Panic-stricken by peripheral visions, earthen children
seek shelters: outcrops, overhangs, tectonic caverns,

thick-skinned trees ringed by weatherpatterns: tempest-
thrashed and sun-faded, sand-blasted and fine-sanded,

wind-buffeted; but that heaving grey-furred Behemoth,
that heaven-roaring Leviathan demonstrating inevitability

is astute as any cantankerous, carnivorous predator, dragging
intuition and auspiciousness in its breathless wake. Shape-shifter,

sensitive to every breath within the longest sentence, sentient
conniver of the frozen heartbeat, that mild liquid-stirring

in the tiniest crevices of resonating matter—yet on these barren
plains, these graveyards of ancient trees and humbled rocks

of dust and regret, the solitude of bone becoming stone,
the living are nothing but shrubs and thickets and thorned bushes,

tumbleweed or succulents inhabited by unsavory arachnids,
spinners of nets and strands and traps, minute jittery midges,

poisonous fungi and lichen spores, eukaryotic molds and
unforgiving gnashing fleas. In the luminous presence of cast—

iron shadows, the microworld becomes a hive, a web-
work of ruts and tracks, pylons and cranes, dirt-grubbing

diggers, piles, and earthdams and yawning cavernous shafts
that stretch into underground wells brimming with life-

saving effluents, vast sprawling crystalline lakes bejeweled
in microbial citizens, three-two-single-celled organisms,

that conjoined sequence of animated lipids forming bilayered
vesicles in generous spore-driven assumptions, to the limbed limit,

the furred-hooks of the root-feeders, the intestinal breeders,
to shorten the distance from the cell to the inevitable shadow,

the pumping bio-valve of the heartstorm, the throbbing heat
of the wartorn, the delving, ever-delving evolving symbiosis.

CRANK-HANDLED

If machination in its primal sense was what led us
into the same spiked jaw traps as the Cucuteni—
who incinerated their own homes before wandering on.

False illuminations, you huff, getting down to knob-
& dial-twisting. *Old. Ancient, I'd say. Hand-cranked,
would you believe? A balancing act even among
the best-bred of the day. The slightest miscalibration
would set it spurting indiscretions, words so base
as to crack granite. There's no real sense in putting
your elbows into it (after all, it's only a child's
plaything).*

       Wrench-spinning, you insist nonetheless.
& not until you strip everything down to cogs, spokes,
sprockets & springs, exposing that frail skeleton,
a crude beast of brass. Miffed, stooped, stumped
over yourself, you discover your own speechlessness.

And then—course, I'll give you full credit—you
cough it up: *Nothing ever came from hydrocarbons.
What is it actually good for, if anything?* & as you rid
your fingers of grease & muck, oily-gluey gunk,
it sputters & rumbles, moans & coughs &
for a tremulous moment it's almost coming alive.

INSTRUCTIONS ON FOLLOWING A CALLING

Even though he knows there's no golden mean, no art
of Zen, nowhere that temperate zone the *chakra* settles in—
no *qi* nudging him closer to the absolute—
watch him slip into that golden morning, stare
into the knuckled face of the sun as his shadow-twin
cuts behind him like she's being obscured.

She's always followed him, his hinged trans-
gression of sinew and bone in black speaks
for herself, says the movement lends words,
an ability to rename the forgotten, to face life's shell;
revives that coalescence within oddments,
stockpiles and fixed things, those voices of reason

in some new moon phase or reclining at a fire,
prodding and poring over wise tomes
to pinpoint where he once stood—navigational
on a curve imagined as a straight line
slicing beyond any looming horizon
unhindered by light or time, but whispering

into that transmutable knowledge:
the tear of an infant or a random mote of dust,
or the fine ends of a tiger's whiskers—indelible,
electrified, inked in the sweep of a simple hand motion,
but mired in those granular human hues of bone,
of carbon becoming diamond, or in the star

billowing into an oven of gold, or into the unrelenting
hands of antimatter (that movement that holds
her together), man and shadow-twin dancing
on the fine threads that spin between illusion
and legend and history and the distance
that is only measured in trees and birds and ghosts.

PULL OF THE GRAVITONS

Now again,

the seas begin to rise; each day the tide falls in closer
reclaiming more of the land, I postulate that soon we

shall have to live on stilts like the Bajau Laut tribes of Semporna
who built their homes on coral reefs in the ocean. Ivan grumbles

as he tries to pull apart the two shells of an oyster to get at
the tender flesh inside. I remind him that oysters are sifters

bivalve mollusks that absorb toxic substances & heavy metals &
that one bad oyster might send him to his death. He huffs, cuts

his finger on the dull knife that slips from his hand, dripping blood
on the rough timber floor. It sits there for a moment in its deep red

as if it is considering where else it might go, until it seeps in
to the old wood, tissue returning to tissue.

Outside the sky

In the distance torn billboards still intrude with their ambition,
with their vivid eyes & the buildings beyond in the deserted

desert city fold & creak in the wind, & at night struts and cables
glow dull in the moonlight like unzipped flies & odd socks.

Ivan hands me the oyster in his bleeding fingers, & I eat it,
tasting the distinct flavors of iron & magnesium & reducible elements

like the ocher I wipe with the back of my hand.
Our past is another now, I say, closing the curtains.

& Ivan? All the smoke has given him watery eyes;

COLD POLLEN

Father built this land from the mud up
with his perfect green hands.

Now, three days on the moor,
nothing to eat and the birds have left us.

Dead crackle of weed as the ground hardens beneath
and the cold sings in our bones.

We know foxes are hiding in hollows and the fish lie
crystal-still on the lakebed, dreaming.

Hunter's shack on the horizon, a crooked tooth whistling
on a hillock. It's rammed shut, padlocked for thaw.

What was it she said?
Something about milkweed to soothe the child that May brings
screaming. I know I should seek it out,
but again my hand returns to that which lies within
and the door flies off in butterflies of rust.

Thirty years ago we settled east, but the moor swallows
the heath as the desert swallows the moor
and the wind grows.

AFTER THE INVENTION OF POLYSTYRENE
A LIGURIAN GOAT CROSSES THE EQUATOR

Abut in a tailspin, mad spark
of keratin scratching hard-
wood—and that buck-

toothed back-bite, double-
chew driving through
everything if-you-pleases:

shoes, hats, buttons, ties—
that crumpled trilby Giuseppe wore
with his '30s Valentino, and

in the buttonhole, an off-
white carnation—in another incarnation,
carrying the fleas of late middle age—;

an idler, a swiller of leftover
orange pop, a guzzler
of misconstrued rubbish, gunk and grease—

sono malcontento e raccattaticcio,
as was parlayed
by Great-Uncle Fabrizzio

before his last hand of blackjack
on an ocean liner
from Jakarta to Genoa via Dar es Salaam

as he observed an empty
can of mystery meat circle
a lone polystyrene container,

then hover and dive gullishly
into a shoal of mackerel
in a calm, whaleless Indian Ocean

crossing the equatorial
with a borderline heart attack
—and finally, that Bornean warrior,

not raised by Cain, but a clan
of cannibals, a bird's delicate leg bone
through his flared nostrils, adjusting

his penis sheath on the crux
of an equinox while dreaming
of a creature he'd never seen

but knew from a lifetime of belly-
aches and breathy sighs, curried
in Bombay on a street stall

in sinews and gristle, fat-
dripping to a chuffed-
up floor, dusted in fine particles

of a most ancient Macedonian gold
collected mote by mote on fingertips
by a team of orphaned ragamuffins

known as the 'All That Glitters'—and
that mad pan-flute-playing
Italian passione that carried

Uncle Fabrizzio from the silver
platter of bright colonial Indonesia
to the shredded and shaded

alleys of serpentine Genoa
in pursuit of a dream of old wives' tales
more than anything he could have foreseen.

BIOHAZARD

Unequivocally yours, Molly—in her last note, she signs off.
It rings in-finite. Toxicity level 4: What we fear but never conceive.

War you tolerate as an acquaintance turned, matter rings in your ears,
crumbled stuff. The virus claims the head, devours the soul,

mal de los rastrojos, breakbone fever, Ebola, hanta, Lassa, mutating
variola.
Things are left standing. In the end we know all their God-fearing
names

like very bad men from the Gestapo, the Stasi. Molly pins them on a
fridge,
beneath magnetized pineapples and smiley faces, beneath Max's
crayoned skyline,

to-do lists, tax return form curling at the corners, takeout menu
from *Wang's Golden Wok*. They secrete through taps, drizzle dams,
slipstream—

like hurricanes we baptize them Alma and Boris, Katrina and
Yolanda
to make them more innocuous for Max. Within a week,

the surgical masks on every street corner, blue and white, then
Gucci pink and Hermes polka-dot, splutters contained behind high
fashion.

And the water we drink is Antarctic ice, eons old—once swilled by
dinosaurs,
an inside joke. Carrier rats bear the brunt, followed by ticks, fleas, lice,

the effervescent tsetse, and we don't swat and shoo—but never the
   monkeys,
our harmless swing-in-the-trees ancestors separated by a single
   strand of amino acid

who've learned to uphold themselves and eat bananas. I say it was
   the dogs,
the Labradors, Alsatians, those ratty Chihuahuas, cuddled, coddled
   and *Tickle Tickle*.

Still, none of it explains away the quakes, the freak storms and
   tsunamis,
none of it justifies the plummeting price of gold, the vanishing of
   the beggars

and the birds, the vacant beehives, none of it. In my mind Molly
   still nags
about that damn tax return. Isn't it strange how you prioritize?

CONTINUUM

We multiply best
in open bodies
with low mass indices
swarm and flock
cluster and conjoin

in dances mimeographed
by mysterious natural
forces undeciphered
faithless phenomena
but orbed ringed

swerved or hooked
collectors congestors
of congenital immunity
diplomatic border-busters
eye upon unwavering eye

one as many as
many as one collectively
as right to civilize
diversity as right

to arithmetic mutation

towards adaptation towards
conceptualization towards
definition and tradition
solidifying in constituents
of a periodic table

as yet uncompleted.

They prisoners
of a singular atomic vibration
high mass index inclined
confounded to expansion
of the straight and narrow

contrive through surfaces
beyond their own layers
in the closed exoskeletons
of their own

devising
matter being matter being

eye to eye too
    without critical observation
        nor mysterious compunction
    but for degenerative
deconstruction that rubble

    may build rubble
        may build rubble again
    each succession wired
into the value-chain
    of being and non-being

        that a creator may
    draw strings and each and every
last one may last
    beyond the great oblivion
        at the end of all things.

DOWNRIVER

Boarding the steamer, we revelled,
you bejewelled, I befuddled,

sky-figured and transfixed in blue,
we: doe-eyed, steered by instinct,

you called it amorous intent,
we trawled for nights churning up fish and weed,

slapping and gulping mosquitoes—until,
wild too, we unleashed

our beasts in tandem;
it was here under a giant amargo tree, fruited

with birds of a single feather,
we dug in, set our traps—

and waited.

TWO

YET ANOTHER REINCARNATION

I pay my soothsayer in hard-boiled eggs, chicken wings,
gristly claws, livers or gizzards—she believes in the due process
of tempests, visions of omniscient butterflies. An old woman
scrubbing floors portends violent crime or racketeering;
finch in the hand, fraud or incest; beetle on the mantelpiece,
ill health. She snatches invisible lassos from the air, spins dizzy
larks above my head, everywhere she sees living dead,
centuries of men on the low road to the county fair, millennia
of citizens ensnared in menial tasks, plowing, sewing, reaping,
daydreaming; mostly she knows where lightning will hit,
who will spontaneously combust, become president,
overnight millionaire. With my own eyes I saw her heal
a cancerous man, the single touch of her arthritic hands.
Twice she foretold my almost-demise, the possible grand curtain,
a lifetime of sighs, once a jet in the skies, once in a train wreck—
she hears the constant chatter behind, grandmothers and aunts and
ex-wives. The past is a series of dots you can trace through the sky.
It's the future that's harder to count, though in a finite universe
only so many spots can branch out—think of it as an astral
   crossword.
And the crowds that shuffle ahead and behind, dead or alive,
all animated beings begging for sound advice on love and career,
sex and disease, there's little she hasn't been forced to hear—
even in this lifetime—so she raises her soul-umbrella,
an unseen parasol, to ward off gnashing thunder of lost voices,
stinging hail of multiple choices; and in her abode of double-
   entendre,
a ghostly breeze blows, two degrees warmer than outside the door,
it snakes under your skin and coils there until you're quite ready
to unravel. The wife thinks I've lost my head in the wild ranting
of this other woman, and she swears by Almighty God the fields
will remain parched and the harvest a washout if I keep this up—

one day she says the earth will buckle beneath my legs
and in my next life when I return as a moth, destined to bump
around lamps, perch still, motionless on bark in broad daylight—
and three days later I shall lay my pearly eggs on the leaf
of an elm, shaded in the gables of a chicken coop, and over
and over, the clucking, the clucking, the clucking.

WHAT MATTER

Cracked skies rain
jellied clusters of tadpoles,
shards of eggshell and feathery tufts,

a sodden box of Lion Brand safety matches, until
we are the only souls alive.
                              Cockeyed.

Like Ivan's suspicious doggy-stares
or reading news deep in the fineprint
of fingertips, the way he inspects crabshell

or those pinpricks of swallows on dog-eared gables,
as if somehow music is alive,
and how he buckles over

to tighten his ragged rope belt,
as if the cord were holding
two halves together

and his left hand, behind
holding them up
on the other side.

MARGINALIA

Stick it to the sky, she said.
Let him have his hell in heaven.
She meant that fingerburned creature,
and he was easy to comprehend
sitting there on the railroad tracks,
biting his dirty fingernails.

And, upon the wet straw,
in that westbound cargo hold, those windseekers,
those twilight pioneers,
she wilted. The Sun was a stagnant bowl
of canned peach slices, and at night
the Moon was a dirty, linoleum-coated tabletop,
and she, tucked in, deep into the well,
deep into the coat
of starlight.

PERCOLATING MAN

Can't remember if ever I was a child who healed like others scrapes
turning

to scabs yearning to be picked and scratched but worming under the
skin like

silverfish Foreign among you I stir in the muddy gravy of the city
growing old

in drafts rubber-soled and checkered in flannel slippers so my feet
don't touch

the bitters and in the dim morning light three roaches in the kitchen
Tiberius

Nero and Marcus Antonius battling over my crumbed dominion of
linoleum

in corners never reached they slip into the walls when I'm frying my
egg and the

coffee in the filter dribbles the marble sheen of cream and the distant
choir

of the city angelic in its own hallelujah until seventeen down a man
with no name

six across a looped rope and the answer on page twenty-nine past the
bombs

the price of fertilizer past the supermarket specials and the saros of a
recurring

eclipse when the umbra doesn't reach the earth past the rattling of
the janitor

on the stairs and behind the walls a million roaches waiting for the fall

of the empire and my stigmata never quite healing over

AMELIA'S ORANGE GROVE

Juan doesn't dare ask, but knows Amelia has others—
in dark cities, in the dust of autumn, pictures her
winding down dwindling alleys where windows
slam shut at noon; sometimes he smells them
emerging from Amelia's pores at night
when she sleeps and he turns, watching streetlight
flickering forgiving forgetting; and
when she's three hours late his heart thumps
like a man jumping from a train, Juan knows—
and it's a knowing like the smell of iron in the air
before rain—and he knows she's tasted that greased-back
ape with the silver tooth, with the diamond ring
and that seaman's tattoo, he who wanders
winking lazy-eyed Friday nights; Juan thinks
he'll be jealous, bubble and sear,
thinks he'll tear himself right down,
separate ego from alter ego,
but strangely he looks out at constellations
trying to remember Sagittarius from Capricorn, searching
for the virgin and sky's dangling umbilical cord;
and Amelia prodding her rice and beans and
garlic rabbit, forking skins right to the edge,
slurping wine on water on wine, telling Juan
her mother has mortgaged them a house
downpaid with the last of Xavier's will, in the Navarra,
and a stream wriggling eels, an orange grove
and a future mother should really be drinking milk
building up the calcium in her hip bones
and wouldn't it be wonderful when they were finally alone
without aunts and uncles and cousins
without nephews and nitpicking mothers
who prod their noses in their affairs,
and Juan peels back his orange layer by layer
and swallows skin, flesh, pips, swallows it all.

MARC VINCENZ   27

GODWILLING

As if a single god-bird might engineer a perfect single egg
upon an outstretched sky as if upon a hand and peer in

dotingly upon its singularly-anointed god-children. As if
its beastly god-children might animate one round world

and venerate the breath of a single, dying sun. As if
they might annotate adolescent tribulations in the name

of god-granted immunity, illuminate vacuum-sealed
darknesses in a germ-free mythology. As if a trillion words

were more iridescent than a throbbing butterfly wing.
As if through the miracle of the internet a single truck

might deliver organically-grown bananas right to your doorstep;
and, godwilling, without infringing a single godly copyright at all.

IVAN SCREAMING BLUE AT THE SEA

That seething you, that Ivan beseeching, teasing rubble from
    random rock,
words cleft in bones & then a pulling like worsted steel from stone,

this stressed strata, this layer cake of humus, crushed shell &
    cartilage, & here
behind the wall—stretching desert to detritus coast along the
    backbone

of the once muddied now ossified earth—

in the mind a crowd still clamors (& with all that finger pointing,
    spitting
& pouting), the sing-song of the *String Him Up!* or, *Stand Him
Down!*

He who inflicted, who switched off the Perpetuum, he who burned
bodies like flat tires (you could see the smoke on the horizon for
    weeks),

he who sterilized for the sake of the children—

Oh, you Shylock, Ivan! foaming in the surf here at the wall's coccyx,
the sea calling you straight into her arms & sand up the nose,

sand spitting up flies & here, finally, I'm yelping over the roar,
I'm trampling the sodden debris. *You can shout all you like!*

Even the wind can't hear you—

You who never squandered, who padded your shoes like nobility,
& in the end, painted with the priest's even breath,

as if immortality might save you from yourself …
tonight the sea whispers below the wind & the feral moon smiles

& once again, in a dimly lit outline of life—

you bend down, picking up the threads that worm in the sand,
you, Crowned King of Seaweed, Ivan screaming blue at the sea.

TREE LUCIDITY

I was taken in by a childless widow woman,
a gatherer of things: the trace of a hand seeking form,
the reckoning of stars, the infallible knowledge of grass.

She taught me how to look on the other side
of the eye, how to cup my hands to hold a dream,
how the tree was a broken line of wind. She was a master

of the forgotten tongue of leaves & broke bread
with the soil so she knew the sweetness of earth
down to its last crumb. She taught me that *time*

was the most common word spoken by man
& often she would wave her arms as if casting spells.
When I turned seventeen she presented me a deity

without a head & a hand clutching a rose
& reminded me that our dreams have only one actor.
She said: *What you read in the oak tree's bark*

is the expansion of light into reason, the will of the man
behind the wall of trees. Search for the woodcutter
who returns to his thoughts in deep dark smoke—

& she sent me out on my way into the old country.

OLD COUNTRY

On Sundays before she rises to the murmur
of ancient god-call, before a thousand pilgrims

plummet, cows graze uphill against the grain.

& as mountain swelters in shadow, the last lynx
growls in the trees. Gian and Giulio guzzle beer

hot, even in the swell of lukewarm summer.

In this hidden valley night crawls slow, here you
find the lost snow of Caesars, the pit that held

a hundred angry Celts roaring at shin-yapping hounds,

bleeding spikes thick as arm-wrestlers. He enters
the shrubbery pelted, without a single thought

for blood, but for lichens & wild crowberries.

She turns to face him in the dark earth
of her precious skin, a fine golden weed of hair

like Cassandra, & asks him to let the wolves in.

BECAUSE OF THE WOLVES,

we're forced to cross this brush—
thorned thicket of interlocking wires,

defense of wars on a rockface
of break-neck spines.

Ivan says he can't comprehend
why of all creatures

the wolf is now at the top of the predator pile.
Organization, I say, ripping my trousers,

wishing I had more than hands
to pry apart these crude defenses.

I look back at Ivan & the branches
push blood into his eyes but he smiles

for somehow this is more real,
truly earthly like breath, like tears.

& behind, pacing, coughing, yelping,
wolves like children would bite down

on any bone to rid themselves of the
pain they carry with them in their teeth,

in their labored breathing.

FOR THE SHADOW COUNCIL,

history has no future   it's more testament than tenacity
more tenement than transience

                             an illusion of Earth standing on its head

like the old codger who collects
in the underpass connecting
                             and the late cars squawking overhead

and what of the rusty cup and the mangy dog?

obligatory for a man who fights for poems by firelight

and she
             never once reincarnated

she who smells of forgetfulness and TV dinners

she who carries the cart to the hypermart for dented cans and cold
cream

and he
             he with the scar under his left eye

the crewcut and the crescent and teardrop tattoo
always crying to the moon
always ready to die

and on the way home to the other side
        where beer was once served lukewarm

she   another she

            carries the touch of men's hair and fingers

filaments of inbreeding breathing through layers and skins

reeking of old men's fables
                        of survivors and war heroes

and though their ghosts have vanished

                            shadows still drag behind like
                            bats

transmuting along the corridors

                        swooping above flagpoles

lining the concourse
with their indelible silence

THE MOST BEAUTIFUL BOOK

(1)

I know Molly would say, *Ask, ask the clouds*. I do, but they remain
lifelessly resolute, waveringly disconcerting. One would think

the dead and their Vitamin B and E would have nourished the soil
all these lean molecular years. There's something like broken egg

filling my head the color of bright morning and I consider
the once-glacier-fed dry riverbed. Clear, clean waters sluiced

into a bay of plenty—days of whales and dolphins and swordfish,
seabirds announcing the medicine of minnow and mackerel.

Now this sea spits and froths green bile along her worn edges, and
tired Max, shadow of a child in a pale greasy-paper complexion,

whose eyes that grasped constellations are grim like industrial smog.

(2)

He reaches up and holds me in a dour cemented glance—
once wide and aquamarine as Molly's—inky hair pressed

to his skull, lank ringlets, tentacles of thought, remains
of innocence worming their way to the surface:

It's all right to cry again, isn't it. He expects no reply, but I say:
We're nearly there, child, back ... (The word "home" is trapped

elsewhere.) From here above the slough, this windbreak
is Ivan's last grip of civilization. His coastal holiday residence,

La Residenzia del Vaticano he calls it, or his domed Papal abode—
least when there's Friday fish for supper: cobbled shack

wrapped in cables and stripped wire, splintered telephone poles,
rusty bricks of air-conditioning ventilators, wastewater drainpipes

and runoff tubes, manhole covers, plastic trashcan lids,
roof hammered in a ragged weed of black polyethylene.

(3)

Metallic reptilian scales resonate a dull buzz—as if the bee, having
sourced its nectar, were transmitting a shortwave dance. The child
   digs
into this wrought-iron shackling—his inside darkening, turning
   outside—

we swab him in rags of frayed cotton. Even now, naked down to his
   last
skin, he grips our meager dinner like an adored wooden toy: a
   locust and
two cicadas: one wingless, one legless, another, the discarded
   crystalline

shell of a nymph—an outer layer hung out in sacrifice for the Great
Provider for the greater good. Ivan boils seawater sifting the surface
   for salt
and scum; *the empty shell, so he says, is shed every seven years as the
   soul*

inside outgrows itself. The Recipe: a barbiturate: salt-sweet female yin
to cool, to dispel the heat within, a tonic to strengthen the qi, *to nourish
the sanguine.* But upon the invertebrate's bodies, the child's fingers,
   vice-like,

as if any moment the dead might fly. In the end, with mini nail
   clippers,
Ivan dissects them little by little, abdomen, thorax, waxy wings—
   only giant
eyes remain firm within the child's grasp, transfixed in a tiresome
   grey light.

(4)

Out here beyond the bluff, approximate angler Ivan,
spear in hand, wades through shallows as if fish might materialize
from sand. Ivan chose this place for his tide—*My tide*, he's often said,

harbors great distractions, incredible knickknacks, unexpected artifacts,
diversity in wood and leather, floating islands of multicolored plastics and
aluminum—the bottle-tops of a billion fizzy drinks, contents broken
    down

into the dead and their unshaking atoms—carrier bags, pots and
    Teflon pans,
other composite materials that float, like buoyant us, singular sturdy
    strollers
for old ladies that shopped, boots that spurred horses, perhaps elephants—

one for each foot of the day to brake the pace of tedium, and, a heart
surging vein to lung to hand, it comes, it goes, it comes round again.
The tide, you see, sifts the enduring from the ephemeral/existential bite

*of dust and sand and fleas—*and, he adds, waving hands—*even though*
they told us they were no more, sometimes: wholesome, unblinking, wide-
gaping silvery fish, not in shoals, not in pods, but singularly alone like us.

(5)

I'm here, Child, I dare, pulling up a chair with nothing more monotone
to voice than: *You're alive*. Sodden Ivan stumbles in, trouser-legs
fixed at the shin with what appear to be pink fishnet stockings:

By the fat Cardinal Mendoza, I've got it! he snorts. My excited stomach
rumbles, anticipating a meaty lunch of broiled cod or harbor porpoise.
Dripping, exhilarated, glowing behind grimy teeth and gripping his gaunt

girth, Ivan says: *Ho-ho-ho. Merry Christmas!* and wrapped and ribboned
in his dry purple seaweed, produces a gift from behind his back—
flashback—Max's blue eyes revive, and with them Molly's visage,

the freckles, the pouty lips. He tears the package, ribbons slithering
from his bed, and although it's warped and bent and fish-bitten, ripped
down the spine, it holds together as if it had been kept alive by Ivan's

personal tide to reach this child's bedside in this particular shack leaning
precariously against this barren shoreline. Underneath a scum of salty-
sandy slime, the book's cover just visible: an image of a disfigured,

grotesque monster half-man, half-beast, like the legendary minotaur
only more comic, sitting sadly alone within a glade of towering trees upon
a grassy pristine shore, and, sailing in from a distance, a single sailboat.

(6)

The day after, it rained. Ivan told me it had been nearly a year and
our clothes and skin reeked of sour ocean jetsam. For fourteen days

and nights it belted, and that same cloud that had stone-walled
the sun all those weeks was blatantly guffawing. Max would have
  spun

and tumbled in these April showers. The cloud had answered
  Molly—
my question had been baited but the mackerel refused to bite.

Max's last words were also a question: *Where are the wild things
  now, Dad?*
Deep in the woods is what I wanted to say. But there are no woods

anymore, and seldom words—only filtered memories washed in
washed out, by Ivan's illimitable, mothering, bookish tide.

SHORT LESSON FROM THE
EGYPTIAN BOOK OF THE DEAD

Before the birds return, the flies—
electro-kinetic pellets flecking

blank walls—devour the flesh
of your simple home in uncountable clusters.

You spin in your spiderweb
of patched cotton gauze, dervish-

summoning the wisdom
of ancestral ghosts flaming

through paper-thin dimensions.
What lurks beyond this breathy realm?

Are you attempting to ascertain those
that do and those that don't belong?

Solidarity may be found even
in the gravestone's faded words.

You on a whirl, bird of passion
performing for shadow cousins,

dust-dreaming-up fog, and the snowfall
of rust and paint and broken nails—

the sound which arises is singular:
a noise, but, no, not music—not quite yet.

MOON TREES, A MOLDERING

Follow me barefoot
into the steadfast motion of days
as the fingers of trees
reach the unassailable
and the sun lingers
waiting for night to follow moon—

until, at least a cloth century unravels
banking upon the shoulders of rivers,
and the roots,
the roots like tapered worms,
settle down into a moldering.

Follow me barefoot
into the rain that embitters
the marsh in cut glass tears
where, the moon trees,
carriers of a sweeter fruit,
grow wild upon the slope
above the grasslands
seeded from the milk teeth of nurseries.

And watch for the blue fern that snags
and the whirring spores
that catch in your hair,
a net cast wide over the world,
and the birds,
again,
making toward heaven.

THREE

WOLFBOY

at the Oxford Medical Convention, 1851

He abhors the pipe-smoke of mansions,
the comforts of carpets and papered interiors.
Surely he is part of the great animal continuum.

Note the raised forehead, the elongated ears.
The wide nostrils. And where is his need for geometry?
for lines and symmetry? His hope for utopia?

And gentlemen, observe the lack of a symbolic imagination.
He hardly knows how to hold a pen.
And paint? He rather eats it—

possibly due to the nutrients he is lacking
from his feral diet of dirt and twigs and wild berries.
Where we meet nature with the edges of our tools

he embraces it, rubbing himself in mud and leaves,
twittering quite happily like the birds.
And we have found, just as a dog with his bone,

he hides all his decomposing possessions in the ground,
possibly for the chance to dig them up and admire them again later.
And he is quite color-blind, unable to distinguish

the fleeting from matters of irrefutable consequence.
Here, gentlemen: let me present to you the living worm
plucked from our dusty book of nature.

WEIGHING THE BROKEN HEART

Blessed the wind. Cantankerous, asthmatic priest
in swollen robes & feathered headgear—
once oceanblue & redgold—now charcoaled

darkening to soot. Waterfed & corn-bred, sun-
worshipping, sun-cursed, a ruinous disseminating
soul, gilded & guilt-ridden, heavy-handed &

lightly-touched—exhales in exhausted prayer
through empty lanes & alleys, prods rooftops,
rattles broken panes, half-open doors, hinges

groaning upon buckling frames, fingers
familiar faces of dying trees, thumbs anemic
birds' nests, rubs eggs to awaken life within,

kicks empty bottles & tins into blank squares,
crumpled things under porticos & steps, blows
ancient news into coppery osprey, kites, puffed up

eagles with giant wings, tears leatherbound
psalms from the palms of pews & aisles,
whispers names of long-forgotten gods, leftover

vowels as if in pidgin, as if in a burning
foreign tongue &, as he gathers himself
from his four corners, draws upon the strings,

he recalls what it was like to breathe
life into sun-filled stuff, how oxygen was
a litany & how every rain was an *Amen,*

he remembers cragged prayers, fragments
in leaves scattering within his own tree, roots
sinking to search for belief, limbs stretching out

over a flock—the tremulous keys of a Portuguese
accordion wheezing a simple song into his lungs,
the exhumation of a thousand jagged sins.

& now, on his last legs, he must remind himself
once & again, he is neither woman nor is he man,
he is nothing, nothing at all. Blessed the wind.

WEIGHTLESSNESS

100 tornadoes in 24 hours
and you tell me there's nothing wrong—
I know the sky brushes inside your head

and the Sun has become unbearably hot,
yet you tell me you healed your family
with the cycles of rising stars—

as if stars had anything to do with OCD,
and your daughter's truck-driver friends
knew anything about Sartre.

It is only in our decisions
that we are important.
It's not always about the matriarch, you'd said,

more often it's about that habitable zone and what you make of it,
how primitive life forms
react to sunlight,

how dinosaurs eventually arise
from single cells,
how creatures like us

learn to take
wind, water, fire and earth
shake and stir, and recreate life in test tubes.

STROLLING INTO THE CLOUD FOREST

> *We always want to see what is hidden by what we see.*
> —*René Magritte*

We've watched them smolder—and yet here's another jigsaw.
Observe this lichen encrusted twig. *Ceci n'est pas une pipe.*
And what the fuck *is* this? Neither pear nor banana is it.
Here, right here, are words from a panopticon of memory:
spiderwebdew, caterpillarleafbites, wileyantattacks.

And would you look there. An infant walking moments after birth.
Isn't this just a living garden of eden.
See those insects converge within a single tangle of latana weed.
The scrubitch mite injects toxins under the skin
as the bleeding heart tree nourishes the Hercules caterpillar.

The faint whispers. That softly softly weeping of waterfalls and
  rapids.

And somewhere the slow
scrub fowl cackles. Up there
nectar-eating creatures
are drawn to sweetness and the purple-crowned doves feed
in the Bollywood tree like off-key movie stars.

Blinking sunbirds hover at panes
and a light mist swirls into the valley.

A flock of red-bowed finches dances
within a single ray of sunlight as we celebrate
something too ancient for us to recall—

it's miraculous we're still laying eggs
amongst the crackling leaves. And again the clatter

of the sulfur-crested cockatoo. Ahead,
knotted and twisted slings of vines. Dead
branches knuckle some kind of termite code.

We begin to understand, don't we? don't we?

But the pigeon's glaring red eyes betray nothing,
and nothing but eyes,
eyes with pointed questions.

IVAN COLLECTS BOTTLETOPS

after Coca-Cola

Lightning-rod white on red,
fist-end of a wizard's swizzle stick,
that All-American red white and you,

like it was scrawled by a Thoreau
sitting on a tree stump overlooking
Walden Pond, beads you down

with its heartbroken redeye
to let you know it's very much the real thing,
would like to teach the world to sing

like all those families
who grew up on the Fixer,
who can trace back generations

to that unbeatable feeling, now floats
on its own coating of carbon-emulsion,
rubber rings and serrated flip-caps—

bowling-pin bottles ground
and reused, shattered, skimming puddles,
returning to the carbon dirt

where Ivan digs them up
with his fingers and curses when they're bent,
twisted or scarred. He hammers them flat

to cover his south wall,
pins them like dead butterflies
to face dust devils, and at night

he smells that ancient brown rust
that once pulverized nails, now spins on them.
A pure sunlight that fizzes, he calls it.

Life begins in the dark champagne.
You really can't beat that feeling.
Twist the cap, he says all the time.

SHORELINES

Sketched
in a single
enigmatic   flourish,
they continue,
these coastal shores
he withdraws,
profiles of limbs
& chiseled faces,
one-eyed guardians,
sentinels peering,
shadow keepers
catching the light,
& that upswell,
that double chin
of land pushing back
against age's
inevitable forces
& that upstart, wind,
Neptune's blind   hand
seeking eyes, nose,
cold-bitten lips
& here and there,
caught in the   polyphyletic   net
of kelp, faded   in iodine,
that old leather
of a boot, a polystyrene
coffee cup,
a green soup bowl,
then a miniature hand,
palm up,
finger curled,
menace furled
pink towards the sun /
red towards the light—
long ago lost,

this crab tree shadow,
this dancing   marionette,
four severed limbs
carried to four ends
by four winds,
cast in its own
mother-image, made
to comfort & console
to contend
with magical love:
and here—Look!—an empty can,
a funnel, and there!
a flash
of broken
mirror holding back
that vicious
cycle of   repetitiveness,
that forever staring
back into time,
preserving   the wave,
preserving   the ex-
halation,   the ex-
trication of
being and   never-
being, of   having
and never   having
of moving into
the ditched
shoring
& that vitreous
yearning
self-contained
in a face
in the flourish
of a cross-hatched
shoreline.

RAW BREED

Here are hearts
fisted like plums,
purpled from civil war,
rough and flawed
and scarred;

and here are birds
like teenagers
row upon row
chirping on bent telephone wires
waiting for fallen fruit;

and here is the gnarled face
of a singed nation
and eyes that cut
asphalt.

On cold moonless nights
at Frank's Hideaway Motel,
perched upon the flimsy rail,
a billowing cliff,
we wash the dead from our hair,

and like those dinner dances long ago
we whisper
and squeeze ourselves
into deep dark corners.

AFTER THE GREATEST WAR

I observe him—possibly as a cat would
a bloated toad among night reeds—
my roasted almond eye reflected

as intention to paw, prod or pry—
and yet he sleeps—or so it appears—
mouth so agape I feel the need

to feed him grains or corns or seed
that he might grind to flour in his sleep.
He is more like papier-mâché

bandaged in his damp, piss-warm sheets—
in his dreams he still licks his wounds
faithfully, faithlessly feline,

nurtures the last face of his moon-willed girl
on the back of a crowded yellow bus—
even among all those pulsing shadows,

she lights up—her mercurial nose,
her chiseled Greek cheek bones,
that quicksilver hair like steel wool

quite ready to be spun into his lovespeak—
and when night flourishes in its colorlessness,
when wind is a labored breathing,

his lids flutter like moths awakening,
his murmurs swell
to old crone groans and moans

which curdle the blood
so thick it barrels
against the inner-ear.

DIVINE

He wakes me claiming he's cracked it,
his turtleshell snapped by fire, mostly

he has hot water bubbling, or wild lichen
tea, hot stones burning in frozen hands;

the mornings here are cold, the air a mist
of snake tongues, the snow doesn't settle

long, melting by midday, turning to mud
& dragging trails under arches and rails,

the ancient bridge that spans Ivan's Ridge,
a rift so deep sound itself cannot escape.

He's tried all manner of geomancy, augury:
The I-Ching, pick-up sticks, chicken entrails,

reading the lightning & rain; apparently
angles say everything: he even pulled apart

our pig's liver with ivory chopsticks,
Herman Hog, a red Duroc, last of its breed.

Now, rattling rabbits' feet and sharks' teeth,
he tells me earnestly he's no false prophet.

You have to learn to recognize the signs,
even a grain of sand has something to say

if you know how to read it, but the turtle-
shell is like an open book, the Shang Chinese

were right, he yells, cupping the plastron plate
in two hands to the light, a wedge of hot gold.

& then he furiously scribbles with a stick
of smoldering charcoal, zigzags & whirls,

triangles & stars & bumpy lines that connect
like single cells multiplying on confluents

secreting from thermal vents & slowly
a pattern emerges, the story of a race

with a myth of a flat world on the shores
of a cosmic sea standing on the back

of a turtle standing on the back of a
turtle—all the way down.

UNFATHOMABLE MAMMALS

You ask the skipper
if there's an oil rig boring out here,
simply anywhere where
molecules congregate to form solids.
Not a blind bean, he says,
smirking planktonic into the
the oldest soup in the known universe—
born of mollusks a million muscles old—
a gazpacho of the mealymouthed:
krill feeders, bioluminescent foragers
and their algal cores, known as seventy percent
of this godless world.
It takes waters from the South Pole
one thousand six hundred years
to reach the North, he says
fingering the wheel with clenched breath,
waltzing in step with *seesaw seesaw*.
Now the waves heave twenty feet high;
we skew at forty-five
as if we are to downplunge. Petrels, terns skim
the troughs; a stray pelican caws, mast-circling.
You've heard in thirty years
there'll be no more fish in the ocean
and yet, today, orca pods roll on their hunt
single-eyeing us, five of them, black humps,
a mythopoeic serpent undulating, penumbrating,
homing in for the slow deadly bite.
You could almost reach across
into this wavewall
and fingerstroke their marble-smooth skins.
Supernatural.

THE PEOPLED POND

That's nothing. On our island
even the parrots speak 4 languages,

yet it's distance that matters in history.
The wider it spreads, the more influence grows.

Oceans are figments of a cartographer's imagination—
wind and current unify tribes, countries, nothing else—

as citizens, we are beholden to trade winds,
wish corn to raise its head

and tell us of our dream metropolis,
for we have built the pyramids

and fantasy has long ago been crushed out of the mind
by tectonic evidence, by our bearers

of messages to the other world
that don't reveal the time—

posthumous solace of canonization,
dark heart of dark leaves

and those waterways clogged with vicious ooze.
Was it all just an explorer's dream?

Was the tongue truly loosened in stones?
Surely, like the Aztecs, we are the beloved

of the snake.
In this next era of 1,728,000 years

are we destined to be reduced to ruins again?
Are we not the god who grows crops,

who makes hay in our own image?
Or perhaps we are the night mice

scrambling between the ears of corn?
And what are those ink blots in the sky? Holes?

PETRIFIED MYTHOLOGIES

At the center, the monkey puzzle
and the scale of seven tones,
those metals forged in the heart of the sun
and their mind-blowing revelations:

The Aztecs said there were 13 heavens,
9 hells of suffering souls
and everywhere legends
of virgin births.

Life as far as we know it
requires life-supporting illusions,
facts of mind made manifest
in a fiction of matter.
If you shake a rattle that sounds like rain,
rain will fall. Celebrate a child's birth
and the earth will bear fruit.

Bury the dead and they shall return petrified
burning in that stark mythological sun
that enslaves us, made us
love gold.

WICKED MOTHER MARY

This caterwaul of well-wishers
has you all aflutter

                    sympathy doesn't really suit you
                    you prefer the uninterrupted

the noise that becomes silence
the churn of your own TV

                    like a laundry machine
                    the tumble and rattle of soap

clattering in the clamor
of false *amour*

                    of diamonds and promises spent
                    and
                    spending on the wicked

lifesavers in perfect teeth
and time is an anomaly

                    a spring, a fan fluttering, except
                    when you cobble yourself together

old leathers sagging, straggling tethered
rolled out to perform miracles—

                    by the bell—down the hall
                    in the holy of holies

Sister Bacon on her rosaries
Mother Marys as you sit there

                    in your solemn grimace
                    trying to get it all out

the garlic, the whiskeys
the endless cups of holy wine, crossed and
                    fingered, sacrificed in liquid
                    the blood, the host

the blathered and sanctified
the right upon rites, the unions

                    of the blessed, the always
                    always immortal, the trying

to get it all out and that holy water
chuckling beneath

                  and when she thumps your chest
                  like she's really angry

at someone else, but actually
because you're forgetting

                  to breathe, the filling of capillaries
                  returning carbon dioxide

to its rightful place
you can't face this, this humiliation

                  expunging more than once a day
                  and you close your eyes

pretending you're crouched
in a tropical rainforest

                  birds purring in the trees
                  sunlight slivers piercing leaves

burning the haze
from your eyelids

                  back in your own room
                  pillow-propped, sipping lukewarm

milk from a straw, but dying
for a glass of Merlot, a Davidoff cigar

                  or even a cheroot, you admire
                  the walls, the goosebumped plaster

speckled in rising nipples
as if you stroke them to attention

                  and the fan whirring on the ceiling
                  sounds like the whimper of a
                  woman

VIEW FROM A BACKYARD

A brief metallic sound:
keys upon coins upon coins upon keys.
She's saying just do it—and,

it's not acidic like some well-inclined logo
ticked for athletic shoes, at least not
until the afterburn quietens

in the inner view—but there is a problem;
these matches are damp and although
she would love to ignite before dusk,

she already blazes in luminescence, exudes
a whiff of adolescence in her wild spray
of indigo blooms. And I hesitate

to let this cigarette tumble, to witness
all this youth go poof in blinding smoke
that waters. Even these crinkled wrappers

and dented cans smack of romance
in our bold designated light, nuzzling
each other like concerned lovers. Behind

the man-holed chicken wire, torn
from hinges, seething, the defensive
warehouse glares—and from nowhere

a soul sensed, not a single woman pushing
a responsibility, not a lone child spinning
wheels, not even a rat's determined squeak

to disturb this angular indifference. Honestly,
what *is* the sound of citizens walking
in a new age of supple soles?

SOMEWHERE AT THE TIME OF ORATION

Those who observe, transcribe; objectify

      that which shall one day stand again

and what is for now, just trace elements, remnants,

      faint odors lingering in immolate gasses

falling star-like into the liquids of a blue world,

      humming within the molecules of his cells—

he who follows the rhyme,

      follows the cadence of vowels and hard recurring noises

rain on wood or steel expanding in solar heat,

      he who has earned the right to dwell upon solutions

as upon the wheat and the corn, as upon the soft wither of skin

      drowning downward like glass returning to its natural state—

seated, but always standing, again and again; and lying

      but always moving forward into the stream of time

to cover distances, to leave but always return,

      to find his connection with the night and all her strands—

those who observe beyond immeasurable distances

      beyond light, in the image of a single word

never to be repeated again.

the never more than promised   the never worked for   Orpheus night-
riding dark matter   Mercury's shoes winging it   these backwater illusions

stories from the ether   at the beginning of art   of music humming before words
the discovery of harmony   *Der Zweiklang* this dual-stream of immortality

your finger paintings   more pipe-dreams than shadows

the never more than promised   than never wanted   the eddies   whirlpools   whirlwinds
pockets of nothingness   drawing you back   the before   the nothing

drawing you back   even as creative impulse stirs   creature comforts soothe
for the moment   you look a picture   familiar in your mother's shawl

that something borrowed you never returned

and we too are mythology   you and I   living on in expectations
history's sing-song   we pray for beginnings   like the Buddhists

who have it down   it's better to live again transmorphed   even if only
as a moth flickering   as a bat-bait changeling   inspiration for gods' wings

the nevermore than promised   never wished for   the once lost

always just beginning   regained again   the once and   *nevermore*

FOUR

RUINS OF A RECYCLED EMPIRE

Scattered. These four-cornered artifacts of fourscore villages
of cities & towns. These scraps & shards of the twisted.

That thought-intent bent into lucky charms: wire-frame giraffes,
elephants, drummer-boys & tightrope acts (tiptoed)—

break-neck straining—an uprooted this-way-that key-chain:
trinkets of stars & half crescents, scythes & hammers

spades & anvils—dragonflies murmuring in wired motion,
that quivering-sprung-stirring, the origami of folded oceans:

those decorative effects unlocking double-barrel security measures
protecting single-barrel names & bricks broken then re-broken

to fit dance halls, steam baths, curved stairwells leading
beneath rose trellises & cracked pedestals looming in side shadows.

EVERY BROKEN BRICK

after Zbiginew Herbert

Under transient clouds the plumb lines of trees
find a straight vein of ore through earth;

and like Foucault (his steady pendulum),
the rhythm of the magnetism

that sings deep in the heart of the dearly devoted,
draws a murmuring crowd.

Those who repair shoes and republics
say they are more than cobblers of old soles

and of old men, believe we are made of blood
and illusion, and carry the acrid symbol of their country

sewn under their tongues. Yet, in the short,
they recall little but that nest of tenderness

and the weight of a sleeping head
upon their shoulder, and in their dreams

our own bumbling prophets come to them,
giving names to men and objects

so they may never perish in the rituals of devotion.
Staring into the broken eyes of a factory,

I cannot help but pray to some unknown creator,
a God who may grant me visions. And I see,

I must become the voice for all things
frozen in silence, to raise a hand, point a finger

and walk toward the sun. And, I'll tell you this:
if I return, I shall bring green apples

and where swallows gather in twisting furls
of grey intention, I shall watch for your white sheets rustling.

FOSSIL

He comes alive again & calls them
ancient crabs & I don't correct him

though I know they're trilobites, he
reaches down & feels their smooth

ossified shells, running his finger
along their ridges & appendages,

their sharp protrusions, moves his
thumb across their compound eyes.

I tell him, like us they could see
in stereo, complex eyes that caught

light into far distances, the first
complex eyes on our planet, & then

he looks sad again like when he
thinks of Tatjana & the creatures

vanish into the shades of grey &
grey & grey into lumps of rock

that fight the sea & he heads along
the beach passing a carcass of a

beached whale torn across the shale
& he walks through the gulls that

tear at the entrails trailing out into
the angry blue & the foam at his

feet whiter than the color of his skin,
whiter than the clouds painted above.

SUPERMOLECULAR

Imagine, then, if you will, that river-flowing free form,
that dapple and glint of light as a blinking
of galactic constellations surfacing in water
then vanishing again and that feline purr
of solar systems running towards the edges
of the known universe—imagine all of this
coursing through your veins
and in your bloodwork.

Imagine the iridescence of unblinking
compound eyes and that wild flounder and bounce,
long, swift legs in high-spring kicks
hopping for sheer delight or for their life
and that Cossack dance, the Hopak, *hup hup hup*.
Somewhere the strum of a balalaika
or the zither *pling* of congregating invertebrates,
the sitar-hum of bird formations, those swirling
geometric patterns like sky runes, imagine.

And imagine, if you will, that wind-driven
equine gallop, shoulder to shoulder herding
across wet grasslands and that regal mane stirring
among the tall grasses, that sway and roll,
the telltale ear-flapping of gentle giants,
under heavy tread the earth turning to packed mud,
and, over there, undulant necks outstretched
kissing the tips of treetop leaves like lost lovers.

And listen for the giggling gambol
and the bounding leaps through the trees and their echoes
all along the valley right down to the lakeshore,
where the whisper of feathers and the whir of wings
breathe life into the air—listen. Here's the chirp
of dusk followed by the *koo koo* of night
and there the soft cawing, the rattle of brush

and somewhere near, that satisfied grin,
as stars cluster in concentric rings
and sun pushes down over a far-flung horizon.

SNAKEBITE

Ivan collected him on the beach, flotsam, washed in
with the tide like the bottle-tops & tin cans & toilet seats
Ivan scrutinizes, wrapped in a raincoat & a furry bathmat

that reads *Hotel Epikourios, A Lovers' Paradise in the Sun*
& his shoes fall apart at his feet & the sand in his shag
follows us in breadcrumbs of mites & jumping fleas.

Little fuckers get into the seat of your pants, into the cracks
between your fingers & toes. Ivan steeps him a weak cup
of instant soup: green asparagus, cucumber and peas.

I notice the red bucket, imagine the boy's a builder
of castles, Prince of the Beachcombers, God of Dead Fish &
Legless Plastic Toys & behind at the stove Ivan whispers:

Joseph, Just take a whiff of what's inside.
& while reptile boy is sipping hot mugged soup,
Ivan pries the rose-rimmed porcelain plate from the bucket,

unleashing a thick grey pungent foam that's enough
to buckle the most intrepid, but we haven't had alcohol
in weeks & he reaches in with his finger, waves it beneath

my nose. It takes a moment, but I'm seeing stars &
winged spiders, antlered snakes, horned fish &
for a moment even the origin of the universe flashes

in streaks & lines & mysterious binary codes.

PSYCHOTROPICS

He says "in the metrozone there's only vacuum

                 & it's hard to breathe—colors once brilliant

become mute, translucent crawlspaces are lined

                 with fungus faces & milk dribbles down glazing
& rails where minnow shoals like silver coins spin

                 heads & tails interweaving courtyards embezzled

in mermaid fountains as roads bump up against trees

                 *

                 & in the cold upwelling streaks drag eddies

as waterways clog with vicious ooze as loose tendrils

         of ragged cloth snag & the yarn unravels into that tyranny

of collective objectives where your feet are so cold

           as blood forgets & your hands don't know where to go
& you call up flashcards in your dream metropolis

               as the burn in your face moves to your throat

where those animal murmurs emerge
             in an eye of vapors seeking toxic sex dreams."

BLACK SKIES

The sun bottoms out
and they rise again,

air-tumbling whorls,
screaming four-letter words.

When our backs are turned
they go straight for the warm blood,

dyeing their beaks
in our carbon dioxide,

clicking their beaks
like mad scissors.

Joseph says their magic is in the feathers,
he calls them quills that ink the skies.

I say, strange they bleed cold.
But ah—respite,

he with the bow and arrow,
he with the eyes

in the back of his head,
he with the illusion of time.

WHERE HONEYSUCKLES RIPENED BY THE SUN FORBID THE SUN TO ENTER

As if light always approaches
darkness is time used up
a spot upon an infant's lung
and the dark towers upon the plains

sticks of temple incense
her smoke your breath your smoke her breath
choking dust of ardent black
angelic furrows of mythical intent

stretching black faces
eyes and pouting mouths and forked tongues
mingle in cloud formations
and time and time again

brother (son) turns towards his own earth
sister (daughter) spills water
and Mother Dear (beloved wife) in the kitchen
weeping and baking bread made of love

for no one

LAST RITES

Today he builds a cairn. Yesterday he draped an elm
in scraps of cloth, enumerated each piece;
& on each, a message of faith or salvation.

Even in his feeble condition, he managed to climb.
From the top he said he could see the spires of a city.
I knew he was lying, but played along.

When shall we head out? I asked.
He didn't answer.
Now, here in the dunes at the coast,

he balances an almost symmetrical pyramid of rocks
with one small pebble the shape of a kidney,
symbol of his surviving organs, his electric eye

upon the sea. When he feels she's ready
he wipes his hands of dirt & sand & dust &
circles anti-clockwise, to counter external

influences he says, & now he's murmuring,
a weak attempt at a tune. It's too far for me
to hear under his breath & the wind has

picked up. Besides, a scrap from the elm tree
has landed in my hand, as if to warn me.
Number 134: Do not disturb the sleeping, it says.

STITCHED UP

Only shriveled bits of epigraphy survive
crumbling scraps from a library of letters

that once lit up faces in the crowd
now propelled by jetsam people

collectors of oddments and the wily
strange mumbling hobos with anagrams

palindromes logograms and morphemes
to seed the reawakening world

                              And one day

as if out of a dream she will approach him
he with the tin cup and the flapping shoe soles

to line her clothes with furred quotations
to ease her experiment in social manipulation

to find a way to stitch up open wounds
with the threads of animals infants and stars

THE SIGN, THE SYMBOL, THE BIRD

> *Lost are we, and are only so far punished,*
> *That without hope we live on in desire.*
> —Dante Alligheri, *The Divine Comedy, Canto IV*

(1)

These are the margins of water, confluence of time bled
through warfare, striving ambition, conquest of religion,

architectural prowess, unfaltering contagion—those in league
with their cousins rallied by fathoms of stars & sundials—

only this time, he is driven out, not by a drug-induced hallu-
cination or a repetitive noise, that Morse code he hears night-

dripping, but—& you won't believe it, by a bird,
an insignificant grey thrushling that skims ahead on his word,

Prroo-Proo, Ivan twitters attempting imperatives in this mystical
song-tongue & there she is, that flash of speckled feather resting

at intervals on threadbare scrub, whistling back in her own marvelous
concoction; stub-winged, she spreads bold, catching sunlight,

then driving soldierly onward, & the bird, says Ivan, isn't trailing
a star—I grind my mind to recall there was a celestial body

leading laden men into Jerusalem—not a ribbon of cirrus cloud,
child-scrawl of an angel, grey spirit veiled in white hair, or a bird.

(2)

I once heard that the honeyguide leads African tribesmen
to their nectar of gold, the honeybird who understands both

the language of men & of beehives, who follows the drone
& after the smoking is rewarded the man's trifle of broken comb—

but this, this thrush, if that's what she is, is more determined,
egging us on, & there is no religion in this, or is there?

Ivan says we are to tread sand, rock, & mud, if so be it.
We flee wasps & wild dogs & along the coast the gull-

screech, the whoop of flocks poking, plunging, piercing, sewing surf-
aces & into the dank interior, through the chitter of Godonlyknows,

eyes wrapped in leaves, beneath the bark of broken trees, & observing
from a distance, the curious cacti on the hills, waving us on …

(3)

... until moon becomes a cataract in the blurred grey of twilight,
& the shrill silence like a rush of oceans, conch shell pressed

to a child's ear, drifts us into fitful sleep, dreams of symbols,
antimatter more than matter, more vision than voice—

Ivan records these illusions in lined notebooks—flashes of latent
philosophy, stirrings from the ether, mixed metaphors & colors

that remind him of before; these are the figments he can recall now,
his older words were stolen by this toxic spring wind that carries

an acid rain, colors like pink & azure & zinc white, fragrances
that harbor space ages: cinnamon & nutmeg & allspice

pepper his lines. Once I followed him to see where he buries his
  dead—
he burns them in sacrifice to unknown ancestors, page

by rip-torn page. & as the smoke flies he sees grim skies
revitalized. Smoke, he told me, is our umbilical cord

to those dark deities—the rising of our intentions, wish-fulfillment,
smoke-knowledge as thought hinders our godlessness.

(4)

& still the thrushling flutters on, dangles, bounces, wavering on twigs,
it's then suddenly I realize, as we emerge from the undergrowth

sweating & dripping, scratched through our faces that Ivan, no
Buddhist, believes her to be the reincarnated spirit of his wife.

He asked me once: *Did you eat your way into this life, like me?*
Did you devour your share of the proceeds of your well intentions?

Or, did you live for something more like love or affections?
Those were the days he still made sense, now mostly little

matters, not the grass, nor the sky, there is no stirring
or yearning, & yet, with nothing left there was still more,

like the thrush, like the sunlight on ice, like the industry of bees.
& once, on a full moon, on a solitary clear night, I caught

a flickering in Ivan's eyes: the face of a child,
the face of a boy, intently listening to birdsong.

MOTHS

(i)

Little unhinges him, even the quakes
rattling through his scant possessions,

the roof crumbling about his ears,
the rust in his hair, the saucers smashing

and beneath the floorboards, the flurry
of rats. Good water is scarce, he says.

(ii)

I tell him water is an infinite commodity,
as if there were still commerce left,

an endless supply in infinite space,
more common than rock,

more common that lifelessness.
Since then infinity has turned over in its grave

and the hairline cracks in the fundament
are showing, even under his eyes.

(iii)

Still he doesn't shed a tear, not for his lost wife,
not when the moths rain down on us at night,

flickering on our shoulders, clinging to our rags.
And when he has good water,

he drinks and drinks
as if this may be his last cup yet.

LANDLOVED

This is the place
you wanted to grow ancient,
out beyond the lighthouse
where the cold is
but another shade of warm
and chill is something shared
and stoked with coal.

Coal burns long and slow
because it was once trees,
and truly old trees are diamonds,
all the oxygen of primal day
compressed into a cold glimmering
bullet of light.

When we share a bottle
of your homemade wine
you hum a sailor's tune
as if to lure mariners
behind the breaking waves
of stillness, comfort
and old, old bones.

There's nothing more divine
than you, old woman,
you and the smell of the sea.

ABOUT THE AUTHOR

Marc Vincenz is British-Swiss, was born in Hong Kong, and has published seven previous collections of poetry: *The Propaganda Factory, or Speaking of Trees*; *Gods of a Ransacked Century*; *Mao's Mole*; *Behind the Wall at the Sugar Works* (a verse novel); *Additional Breathing Exercises* (bilingual German-English); *Beautiful Rush* and *This Wasted Land and its Chymical Illuminations* (with Tom Bradley).

He is also the translator of numerous German-language poets, including: Erika Burkart, Ernst Halter, Klaus Merz, Andreas Neeser, Markus Bundi and Alexander Xaver Gwerder. His translation of Alexander Xaver Gwerder's selected poems, *Casting a Spell in Spring*, is to be released by Coeur Publishing. He has edited various anthologies and selected works of other poets, including Hugh Fox's last and posthumous collection, *Primate Fox*. He has received grants from the Swiss Arts Council, ProHelvetia, for his translations, and a fellowship and residency from the Literary Colloquium Berlin (LCB). His own work has been translated into German, Chinese, Russian, Romanian and French.

Marc is the publisher and executive editor of MadHat Press, *MadHat Annual* (formerly *Mad Hatters' Review*), *MadHat Lit* and *MadHat Drive-By Book Reviews*. He is Coeditor-in-Chief of *Fulcrum: A Journal of Poetry and Aesthetics*, International Editor of *Plume*, and serves on the editorial board of *Open Letters Monthly*. He is also Director of Evolution Arts, Inc, a non-profit organization that promotes independent presses and journals. He currently lives in Cambridge, MA.

ACKNOWLEDGEMENTS

Fourteen Hills: "Transmigration"

Washington Square Review: "Snakebite"

The Canary: "Weighing the Broken Heart"

St. Petersburg Review: "Divine"

Plume: "After the Invention of Polystyrene a Ligurian Goat Crosses the Equator"

Plume Anthology: "View from a Backyard"

Manhattan Review: "Short Lesson from the Egyptian Book of the Dead"

Altered Scale: "Static," "Raw Breed," "Ivan Screaming Blue at the Sea," "Continuum"

EgoPhobia: (translated into the Romanian by Marius Suleac),
"Ivan Screaming Blue at the Sea," "Continuum," "Imago"

Zon@ Literara: (translated into the Romanian by Marius Suleac), "Raw Breed"

Connotation Press: "Moon Trees, a moldering," "Pull of the Gravitons," "Imago"

Exquisite Corpse: "For the Shadow Council,"

Brink Magazine: "Wolfboy"

Crab Creek Review: "Marginalia"

Tears in the Fence and *TRUCK*: "Yet Another Reincarnation"

Up the Staircase: "Amelia's Orange Grove"

PIF Magazine: "Unfathomable Mammals"

Caper Literary Journal: "Old World"

Full of Crow: "Cold Pollen"

The Green Door: "Biohazard"

Monongehla Review: "Wicked Mother Mary"

THIS Literary Journal: "Downriver" and "Startwisted,"

Pirene's Fountain: "Black Skies"

Atticus Review: "Fossil"

Frostwriting: "Landloved"

Dublin Poetry Review: "Ivan Sinks into the Honeycomb"

"For the Shadow Council" and "Black Skies" appeared in
The Propaganda Factory, or Speaking of Trees
(Argotist Books, UK, 2011) and (Spuyten Duyvil, USA, 2012)

The following poems appeared in the chapbook *Pull of the Gravitons* (Right Hand Pointing, 2012): "Pull of the Gravitons," "Percolating Man," "Because of the Wolves," "Cold Pollen," "Black Skies," *"Startwisted,"* "Imago," "Psychotropics."

"Supermolecular" appears in the anthology *RHINO: In a Vanishing World* (Poets Printery, South Africa, 2012)

"Imago" was published in the anthology *Otherstream: Shadows of the Future* (Argotist Ebooks, 2013 / MadHat Press, 2014)

Audio versions of several of these poems have been broadcast on Radio Caroline.

CPSIA information can be obtained at www.ICGtesting.com
Printed in the USA
BVOW08s2254180416

444711BV00001B/1/P